WHUT

EXPECT THE UNEPECTED

◆

◆

◆

COLLECTED WRITINGS
MARIAN KELNER

Author may be contacted at marian.kelner@gmail.com

Printed in the United States of America
First Printing, 2016

ISBN   978-0-9969719-5-9

Book and cover design by the Ginger Cat's Booksmyth
Press of Shelburne Falls, MA 01370 [www.the-
booksmythpress.com]

Also by Marian Kelner

As a Sailboat Seeks the Wind: Collected Writings

May We Be Like the Penguin: Collected Writings

CONTENTS

Abduction

The Mother of All Anxiety,
an intra-psychic bartender,
shakes my mind into a cocktail
of mistrust and worry.

The Father of All Punishment
exiles me to beliefs
of indifference and neglect.

These forces are too strong.
I surrender.

How can I do this?
Me in this miraculous body
with a miraculous brain,
an offering among infinite offerings
from the universe that gave birth to me
with such care, such hope.

Airborne

Kate Sorkatchian, the social worker at the Sweet Blossom Nursing Home, was bored. After twenty years of leading simple line dances, calling out Bingo numbers, conducting holiday songs, and teaching simple card games, she was actually almost catatonic. Over the years, she had attempted to introduce stimulating activities, like interactive video games and competitive bocci ball tournaments, but every creative idea had been squelched after Henrietta Goldstein's unfortunate trip down a water slide.

It was now getting close to Kate's retirement and her boredom was making appreciable inroads into whatever sense of good judgment she had left. This became clear when she decided to create a stage diving event in the Home's recreation room. She would hire a punk band and strong young men and have the residents experience flying off the stage and being passed one by one over to the refreshment table.

Kate knew it would take secret construction in the middle of the night and would most likely lead to an earlier retirement than she planned for, but the brain cells that could have put a stop to this were fast asleep and besides, at this point, she couldn't care less.

Ms. Franklin, one of the younger and spryer residents of the nursing home, was the first to be catapulted off the stage. The music was so loud that Franklin used every muscle memory from her days as a gym teacher to take to the air with her hands over her ears. When she reached the top of her arc, she found herself looking down into the dazzling blue eyes and strong arms of a handsome young man and broke into a smile of pure delight. Once caught, she was handed down the line over the astonished upturned faces of those in wheelchairs and deposited by the punch bowl, dazed and utterly thrilled.

This event of course entered the mythology of the Sweet Blossom Nursing Home. The surprise was that the video of Ms. Franklin's airborne trajectory was posted on Facebook and went viral. As a result, stage diving is cropping up at nursing homes around the world. So far there have been no injuries or deaths, just thrills and rejuvenation and the revelation that this indeed is one of the experiences many want in their golden years.

All in a Name

No one knows exactly when my mother's household objects started to move from their designated places and journey elsewhere, but almost everything in the house had. It was becoming obvious that the heavy Victorian sofa, a couple of mahogany end tables, and the prep table in the kitchen that was bolted to the floor were the only things to remain where they always had been.

I first took notice when I visited last November and saw that behind the bathroom door, where I had left the label *These are bath mats*, there was now a wash cloth and long-handled loofah, and when I turned on the switch labeled *bathroom fan*, the essential oil atomizer above the toilet sprayed eucalyptus scent high into the air.

My mother and I had labeled many things in her house as her memory faded, but this was now useless since she was disregarding the entire system and creating an entirely new one in which one word consistently meant something else. My mother claimed she was honing her mental acuity by learning new connections between objects and the labels she chose to represent them, but so far we have seen no evidence of that.

In fact, her exchange of objects and labels has rapidly become a problem, the most recent being when she dipped medicated Q-tips into a cup of hot water because she had moved the tea label into the medicine cabinet, and when she used a small plunger, now labeled *pasta stirrer,* while making sauce as holiday gifts.

We knew something had to change, but so far nothing has except our family games which have changed from Bananas and Trivia to being quizzed by our mother as to what object she is thinking of when saying any given word such as *fork*.

Animal Human Connection

Humans and animals . . .

reproduce
protect and raise children
find food
problem solve
are aware of the environment
create and protect their homes
are aware of danger
communicate
have families
have social systems
claim territory
have emotions
sleep
eat
defecate
groom
mate
play
work
cooperate
travel
have favorite foods
follow routines
struggle to live
try to avoid suffering
have hierarchies
are aware of death
use tools when necessary
have language

At the Edge of Our Worlds

We meet at the edge of our worlds
under the pines pulled high by the light.

Seeds scattered on the snowbound earth
await you and the rise to branches brittle with cold.

How blessed we are,
you with this food,
me with the beauty of you.

The Attic

I

When my twin sister, Morgan, and I were eight years old, our mother went to work, and from that time forward during the week, Morgan would make dinner and I would wash the dishes. We weren't latch-key kids because doors weren't locked in our small 1950s New Jersey town. We walked home after school down modest, tree-lined, lower middle class streets, changed clothes, and snacked on whatever we could get our hands on, especially peanut butter dipped into Marshmallow Fluff. A little before five, Morgan would start dinner.

One day, a neighborhood friend, Morgan and I were in the attic playing hide and seek. This attic consisted of one room surrounded by unfinished flooring of cross-beams and slats. It was dark and creepy in the beam area, but despite warnings, we'd venture out and circle the room with a flashlight. The beams smelled musty and the way was treacherous. Our mother, who worked as a secretary and bookkeeper for a uniform cleaning factory, would soon be walking through the door.

I was on the beams and, in my rush to hide, I tripped over a thick wire, fell forward, and my right foot plummeted through the slats until I couldn't see my leg anymore. When Morgan found me, she started laughing so hard she could barely tell me not to move before darting downstairs to determine which room I had entered from above. It turned out to be our parents' bedroom which now had plaster splattered across the floor and bed.

After cleaning up as best we could, we strategized as to how to break the news to our mother. We would greet her at the door telling her we had made a special dinner and that there would be a surprise afterward that we were keeping in her bedroom. We would take her coat, lead her to the kitchen, bring her slippers, and serve her food while being casual, friendly, and talkative. After stalling was no longer an option, we would walk her to the room where everything appeared perfect until we directed her gaze upward so she could contemplate the large round hole in her bedroom ceiling. We executed this plan perfectly. She didn't get angry and she didn't blink an eye.

II

Fast-forward to high school and Morgan is experimenting with vodka. In true scientific fashion, she keeps drinking to see what will happen, and, what happens is, she's suddenly so drunk it seems best if she were stowed in the attic. I lead her to the stairs and she manages to crawl to the top, but once there she collapses to the floor and immediately announces she needs to use the bathroom. Time is of the essence so I prop her into a seated position on the top step, stand in front of her to make sure she doesn't gather speed, and bounce her on her butt from one step to another. I then drag her by her feet across the linoleum kitchen floor and into the bathroom just as the front door opens and my father cheerfully shouts hello.

This time it is my father being led into the kitchen and me trying to keep his attention away from the sight line, but soon the bathroom door creaks open. Our heads pivot simultaneously as Morgan tries to walk nonchalantly past by pressing her shoulder against the wall for support. A few steps and she slips to the floor. My father doesn't blink an eye, and though concerned, he too doesn't get angry.

III

The stairs to the attic held a significance all their own. Our older sister, Liz, lived in that attic room. She was not known for putting things away and she and our mother were arch enemies. Liz would routinely fill the stairwell with so many clothes and belongings, it became treacherous to go up or come down. Our mother would tell her to put her things away and Liz wouldn't and they'd scream and periodically our mother would heave all her stuff over the railing of the back porch into the yard below. This piling up of stuff, screaming, heaving, picking up, piling up, and screaming ended only when Liz left for college.

These stairs were also a stairway to heaven. In the spring, summer, and fall, we would climb onto the desk by the two front attic windows, climb out, and sit on the roof with the branches of old maples swaying in front of us and the view of the sidewalk and street endlessly interesting. The stairs also became a demilitarized zone for me as my sisters became close and hung out talking and laughing upstairs while I rambled around downstairs. Those stairs came to symbolize the distance I would have to travel in my psyche and life to reunite with them.

The Bend in the River

There is a bend in the Green River where the river changes shape and depth daily. The rocks on the bottom grind their way from one side to the other carving out the earth until trees topple. The current is swift and dazzles in the sunlight.

I visit this bend every summer with my dog friends and see how the winter storms and spring floods have rearranged the landscape. This place is idyllic. No signs of humans evoke a year or a century. Only the sounds and sights of rushing water, of birds, of trees suffuse the summer's light.

I always walk here with a dog, through the woods, across a meadow, and down a sandy path to the water's edge. First, it was with my beloved Pilar, a small Jack Russell/Corgi mix with the brains of a genius and a loyalty and attention I have never experienced before or since. Pilar was a great swimmer. Her lungs took up most of her body so she would glide like a regal ship atop the water, her bent white tail a sail behind her. I could see her legs as she swam by me, her kicks purposeful and able to turn her around on a dime.

Molly, a Springer Spaniel, also loved the water and one of the best days of our lives started at that bend in the river. It was a quintessentially perfect summer morning — the sunlight having traveled all those miles through space to touch us at precisely the right temperature. We swam at the bend and then walked downstream on the riverbed. The land on one side was flat and wooded, on the other it rose like a huge sandy wave. We could hear only song birds and the rush of air over the wings of hundreds of swallows who had made holes and then homes in the eroding sandy embankment.

When I wonder what my last memories will be, I hope I remember these.

Burned

My friend's house
burned to the ground
in an early spring fire,
trees singed, one cat missing.

What to do when there is
no door to walk through
no refrigerator to open
no piano to play
no clothes to wear
no bed to crawl into
no photographs to remind you
of what once was.

Gone this fairy tale of a house,
built with friends, the peak so high
heat lived there in winter,
while she lived below
in 40 degrees
the wood stove blasting,
the stone fireplace blazing.

Now she rakes and sifts,
nose behind a cotton mask.

Do you know what a melted piano looks like? she asks.

Look! she exclaims—
    the photos of Jews being led to crematoriums survived the flames!
    my singed paintings look even more beautiful
    the charred poems left their most important words.

It's amazing, she says.
    Most of what remains is what I've given away.

Change of Consciousness and Climate Change

Many economic and scientific ideas are being presented to address climate change, but they are not enough because these ideas arise out of the same belief system that created the problem in the first place. Albert Einstein's observation that "[no] problem can be solved at the same level of consciousness at which it was created," supports the need for a significant shift in our present cultural paradigm in order for the Earth to re-establish the balance that existed before human interference.

Climate change has arisen from the belief that we are separate from and superior to other species. This misperception has led to the shredding of the web of life on which all living beings depend. If future generations of any species, including our own, are to survive and prosper, this prejudice must end.

We can no longer view forests, wetlands, deserts, rivers, and every other ecosystem as merely sources for profit and products; rather we need to recognize them as the homes to the countless numbers of living beings who weave the interdependence of life. Honoring the rights of these ecosystems and their inhabitants to exist and prosper is key to their survival and our own.

Climate change will be addressed effectively when our attitude changes from everything belongs to us and we can do whatever we want to, as Native Americans have stated, we are a strand in the web of life and whatever we do to that web we do to ourselves.

If we can wed this understanding to our spectacular technological abilities, we will clean up the mess we have made. We will get plastics out of the oceans and purify the air, land, and water we have polluted. We will restore large areas of the Earth to their former self-sufficient eco-systems in which beings large and small, seen and unseen, can once again live in balance.

With this level of consciousness—new to Western scientific culture—we would acknowledge that our belief in our separateness from the other miraculous, marvelous forms of life is wrong. We would apologize for the harm we have inflicted and also celebrate the amazing human capacity for innovative solutions. We would find spiritual sustenance and connection as we reunite with our family, the family of all living beings.

Circling Sylvia

I met Sylvia in the 1970s, when I was in my early twenties and she was in her late forties. I first saw her in the New School library where she helped with research and orchestrated her bevy of lovers. She was beautiful and a rebel to whom shoplifting was a badge of honor in a capitalist society. She was also a marijuana aficionado, and a woman who felt sex was the most compelling activity in human experience. She stayed active and true to these traits until she died at the age of 92.

Sylvia also couldn't stop talking and suddenly my quietness, which had so far been a liability, became an asset. If I didn't say much, it was fine, but I became motivated to push my voice into her monologues instead of remaining completely silent. I found I could say anything and Sylvia would became involved in any subject I brought up until she was pulled, as if by a mighty underground current, back into her own stream of consciousness. She thought I was wise and loved me and I loved her too.

Our lives soon took different trajectories and, by the time she died in her West Village apartment, owned by the man who wrote "Rudolf the Red-Nosed Reindeer," we spoke only a few times a year. I kept putting "call Sylvia" on my to-do list, but postponed calling time after time. When I finally dialed her number, there was a forwarding number. I dial again and her daughter answers. "Sylvia died last week," she said. I can't quite believe it.

I receive an email invitation:

Memorial - Wake - Get Together - *ALL ABOUT SYLVIA*

*In honor of her (self-described) Jewish stomach
and Celtic heart
there will be appropriate food and drink including
Potato Latkes and Champagne*

*So please come and tell your
favorite Sylvia stories*

Her daughter's loft is filled with people of different ages and races. The table has an abundance of delicious food. People who haven't seen each other in years embrace. It feels like one big close family with Sylvia as the presiding, though materially absent, matriarch. The stories begin.

—

One year, Sylvia was preparing a Passover Seder, and she handed me a bag of marijuana and told me to make pot brownies. I hadn't made them before, so when I stirred a little marijuana into the batter and it disappeared, I thought, I didn't put enough in. I added more and the same thing happened, then more and more until I could actually see the leaves in the mixture.

When the guests arrived, we invited them into the kitchen for a taste and soon took our places at the table. The effect hit simultaneously about 15 minutes later and any awareness that this was a Seder vanished. People moved in and out of different rooms to talk in small groups before wandering away as in a Fellini dream sequence. That Seder never happened.

—

Whenever Sylvia went into a store, she had to take something. Once she asked me if I wanted a steak and I said yes, so we went to the grocery store and the butcher handed us a steak and Sylvia told me to put it under my shirt. I was young, so I did it, but my shirt was getting bloody, so I took it out to give to her, and the manager saw us and accused her of stealing. Sylvia put up such a fight that the manager gave her a second steak for free just to get rid of her.

—

Sylvia was brilliant. She had 8,000 books on the most amazing variety of subjects and she had read most of them! We had discussions about everything! And she was socially conscious too. She once worked as a bookkeeper in an off-Broadway production company, and when the bosses changed the number of tickets sold so they wouldn't have to pay the actors their fair share, Sylvia just changed the numbers back.

—

Sylvia had rented a cabin in New Hampshire, and a couple of friends and I were up there and we took some acid, and I remember one of our New York City friends walking across the porch in front of us, silhouetted against the dark sky, saying how she couldn't stand the silence and that the air was too clean. Meanwhile, Sylvia was absolutely quiet and I couldn't stop talking. It was as if we had switched psyches, and I thought this must be how she feels: if I don't say everything that crosses my mind, it's not real.

—

These were unlikely stories at a memorial service, especially for a 92-year-old, but they were all true. The photographs showed her spirit: Sylvia as a wide-eyed two-year-old looking eagerly out at the world, Sylvia as a stunning young woman, a beautiful older woman, then as an old woman with no teeth and a cane. In each one, she had a sparkle in her eye.

Conversation Overheard at an Art Opening

—Don't read that artist statement to me, Collin! It'll ruin everything!

—But this one's good.

—Art has its own voice and it's not pompous verbiage.

—That's true, but...

—Why does she need to elaborate on rusting iron?

—Well, it says here, "Since I was a child, I have loved these reminders of the Industrial Revolution and its lost elegance. These artful shapes reflect the primal fondness humans harbor for natural forms and give a nod to nature as it rapidly disappeared in the face of mechanization."

—Hey, there she is in that aluminum tab dress!

—Maybe she should rust and call herself art! I'm going into the sticks and stones room.

—Hmm, I like this.

—Me too. I used to make little towns out of them in grammar school.

—Did they mean anything to you?

—No.

—Well, here it says, "Sticks and stones reflect a confluence of solidities illustrating the flow of life through millennia while illustrating that water patterns reflect all life regardless of water content."

—I rest my case.

—Oh, this is good. "Though warmth is associated with wood, and cold with stone, hold a stone that has been in the sun and wood from a damp basement and experience preconceptions evaporating so fast time itself cannot be measured."

—Okay, that's it. I'm gonna sit on that hot stone in the corner and make my butt burn and then write a statement on the significance of what comes out of it!

—Whoa! I've got to see this!

Corporate Men in Ties

Their heads pop from tight shirt collars
like round white mushrooms.

Their bodies appear
out of the darkness
in board rooms,
political institutions,
places of privilege and power,

where they spread
their spores far and wide.

A Damsel in Distress

Is there a damsel in distress?
A damsel in distress?

This was my childhood mantra
ala Huckleberry Hound.

I heard many calls for help.
My mother's for one.

The voice I did not hear
was my own.

Dear Family and Friends

Dear Family and Friends,

The time has come for me to say goodbye, at least for now. I can no longer tolerate the small world I have created for myself, and am therefore embarking on an adventure of unknown duration. I will be riding camels and elephants from Ethiopia to South Africa, avoiding every paved road I can with a guide who has completed this route successfully eleven times.

I have met with the surviving nine people who have taken this journey, the other two having met untimely ends, one slipping in the bathtub and the other accidentally setting herself on fire while making pancakes at a church breakfast. I mention this to remind us, myself most of all, that death can come anytime—in the heart of darkness, as Joseph Conrad wrote, or on a sunny morning with the smell of fresh coffee in the air.

My weariness grows with every walk down the groove I have worn from my bedroom to the bathroom to the kitchen to the back door. I want to trod in places few people, if any, have been, to lie under the stars, to hear the calls of monkeys.

No matter what happens, know I was happy and proud to have chosen this path. As the wonderful Mae West once said, "You only live once, but if you do it right, once is enough." In my remaining years, I want to do it right.

With love and wishes that all your wildest dreams come true,

      your very own Frederick

Dogs, God, and the Pope

Brothers and sisters, we are gathered here today in the name of Jesus Christ, Son of God, holiest of the holy by the Grace of God and all that is sacred unto Him. Amen. Sister Mary Francesca Hildegard has called us together on this fine day to bring to our attention a matter of great consequence to our congregation. Sister Hildegard, please come forward and share with the brethren what is in your heart and troubling your soul.

Brothers and sisters, you have known me for almost a lifetime and you know I try to speak only when I feel God is moving through me. Well, God is moving through me now, sing His praises. Amen.

Amen.

Yesterday morning I was walking up to the door of Sister Margaret's house to bring her some egg salad and jello as she will not leave her house after seeing her dead husband standing by the mailbox these 20 years after leaving this world for the better one awaiting us all. Well I came upon a small dog peering from under her magnolia bush with the plaintive eyes of a long-lost child. I offered this dog some egg salad and as he crept toward me I saw a message attached to his collar on this very paper I have here in my hand. It says, "Comfort the afflicted and afflict the comfortable." I felt in my bones that this dog was a messenger from God and I have brought this message to church today so we can decide what to do next. That is all I have to say right now. Amen.

A man sitting in the third pew on the right stood up and said, "I heard that commie socialist Pope in that funny-looking yarmulke say that the other day. I didn't mean to listen to his claptrap, but I was switching channels trying to find that Robertson guy and the remote stopped working and the TV came to a halt as that crazy Pope—pardon my language—was saying that very line. I couldn't change the channel so I turned the TV right off and went to look up that word afflicted and I must say I personally felt afflicted by his comments. I thought I'm sort of comfortable and he was putting the devil's curse on me somehow and I'm asking for a blessing right now. Amen."

A woman in a floral dress and floppy hat who had been fanning herself faster and faster as the man spoke stood up and said, "I don't know what's gotten into me. I truly don't. I know that a man is not to be contradicted, but I can't help myself, may the Lord forgive me, but I feel that dog and that Pope were sent here for a holy reason. God works in mysterious ways, we all know that, and I do believe we truly need to help the afflicted, like poor Johnny with half a brain and a heart of gold. I say we take up a collection for him right now and do a bit of that comforting the afflicted, so help me God."

Mrs. Johnson's guide dog piped in right then and there and a chill swept over the congregation as they collectively began to think God was speaking to them through dogs and that the Pope had something to do with all of this, though they couldn't figure out exactly just how yet.

Drying Clothes

Long ago in my backyard
on clotheslines stretched
from house to trees,

I pinned wet clothes
with wooden pins
and rolled them
slowly
away from me.

Now dryers turn,
the clothes so soft,
a walk downstairs
after dark,

where with warm clothes
against my face
I breath myself
back to the place

where clothes once swayed
in a summer's breeze
as we played
beneath
the maple trees.

Emotional World of Slugs

A yellow slug lies crushed
on the garden pathway.

Two slugs crawl in a procession
around the fallen one,
then over the body.

One tries to raise the dead,
pushing her head under
to bring the body back into life.

Hours later,
the body, drying and shriveling,
is being eaten by ants.

One slug stands guard
beside her loved one.

Expect the Unexpected

My sister Morgan and I buy plane tickets way in advance—a whole lot cheaper and so many choices for the perfect arrival time. Yay! We'll leave on the first flight with only carry-on bags and land in Albuquerque at 11:30 a.m., zip over to pick up the rental car, and be in Taos by early afternoon with a whole day on the mesa before us

We drive to an airport motel the night before, up at 5:00 a.m. and at our gate with plenty of time. The plane taxies out to the tarmac. A certain moment comes when everyone on a plane knows they aren't going anywhere anytime soon, so it was not a great surprise when the pilot signs on, clears his throat, and announces that the hydraulic pressure light is on—one of five—and though this really doesn't mean much, the FAA will not allow takeoff and we have to return to the gate and connect with other flights.

Every seat in this plane is taken. We all collect our belongings and file slowly back to the waiting area where we're at the mercy of one airplane representative trying to figure out 250 connections. Everyone—except me— appears optimistic. My sister cracks open a snack, others are talking. I'm staring at that one man willing him to work faster. The first connection to New Mexico is given away and the next flight is seven and a half hours away. I approach the desk one last time and am told there are two seats on a flight to Denver with one possible connection to New Mexico and that plane is leaving in five minutes.

My sister and I grab our bags and run thinking at least we were going west. The flight is smooth as silk and we think maybe we'll rent a car and drive south instead of waiting four hours for the connection. This strategy evaporates upon hearing the enormous fee for a one-way dropoff, so we track down another airline agent who says we can leave soon if we fly first to Las Vegas, then Phoenix, and then Albuquerque, and I, who until then had a fear of flying, opt for two more takeoffs and three more landings.

We arrive in Albuquerque in the dark and drive north close to midnight. The burrito at a roadside stand in the balmy high-desert sage country helps a lot and I realize I've lost two things: my fear of flying and expecting anything to go according to plan. Other unexpected things of course were to happen, like floating naked on a tube down the Rio Grande between herds of big horned sheep, being pressed down by a heat wave, and finding out the directions to keep going straight and down a hill really meant going straight and plummeting down a dirt road with no railings on the edge of a cliff at a 70-degree angle into a gorge with cars the size of small ants below.

Nothing really ever is as we expect—somewhere in our psyches we all know that—but there are varying degrees of discrepancy, and when that degree is glaring, we're thrown into the moment, and, in the best-case scenario, surrender to it, remembering the only thing we do have control over is how we handle it.

Facing Fear

The warm morning air
slides through the open door
carrying smells of great interest.

My cat, Mouse, does a visual check,
smell test, and 360-degree auditory check,
before bolting outside.

For all her preparation, minutes later,
the upright tail of a retriever
sails by the dining room window,
and Mouse, now four feet up a tree trunk,
expanded to porcupine proportions,
is emitting guttural and unearthly wails.

The dog loses interest and leaves.
Mouse skulks home and hasn't been outside since.
No dog has shown up for months, but
one could, and Mouse seems to be willing
to stay inside for the rest of her life, just in case.

Today is so sunny and beautiful,
I coax Mouse to the door once again, and
look straight into her beautiful green eyes,
murmuring, "It's okay, Mouse. It's okay."

I see the moment she takes my word for it.
Out she goes——then back to the door,
now over to me sunning in a chair,
inside to her food bowl,
outside into the yard, back to the door,
outside, and then in for the day,

to rest from this world of endless danger
and the possibilities of what could happen next.

Family Ecosystems

My twin sister,
six pounds four ounces
dark hair, light brown skin,
a delicate, cheerful baby.

Me eight pounds six ounces,
blonde and crying.

"Such a big a baby," I was told so often,
it has taken me a lifetime to realize
I was four pounds less than my cat weighs
and my cat is not that big.

Upon arrival at home,
my older sister takes a look at us
and chooses Morgan and suddenly
they become the twins.

Like two populations of the same species
evolving in different parts of the world,
they grow into similar facial expressions and mannerisms
while I devise survival mechanisms all my own.

They are still mistaken for each other.
I am still looking for someone like me.

Five Senses

I don't have much sense at all, let alone the ESP, but the five senses, God knows I've got those real good. In high school I could smell Melinda's perfume coming through the sulfuric acid in chemistry class. And touch! Nine point eight on the Richter scale when her arm touched mine.

High school was heaven for a boy like me. I didn't get into the academic stuff, but I aced the senses. My ears rotated like a cat's when Melinda was whispering to her friends, and when I picked up my name and it was connected to hot or cool, I was sure the universe would turn out real good for me, but then, it didn't.

After that football injury, Melinda lost interest and went off to college as soon as we graduated. Now I drive a concrete mixer out to the construction sites on I-81. And that sixth sense you mentioned. I just don't have it. I'm more like the concrete coming out the back of my truck. I turn to stone real quick.

I'm really concentrating on the sense of taste now that there's that new brewery in town. Thirty-two different kinds. And I can taste the memories from my football days. See, there's a metaphor. I was always good with metaphors, so maybe there's hope, a crack in that concrete. Maybe a small flower will grow. Maybe its name will be Melinda. Who am I kidding? But I always was an optimistic guy.

Florida Has an Edge

Florida has an edge
my sister says.
I don't quite understand

until I suggest,
"Let's go see the manatees,"
and find them seeking warmth
in the murky waters of a nuclear power plant;

until I'm surrounded by storks
dropping like high-powered needles,
stabbing fish and flipping them back
into the darkness of their feathered bodies;

until my bike gets caught in hidden sand
and I fall next to a faded sign: *Danger. Alligators;*

until the quiet of an idyllic nature preserve,
is pierced by a child shrieking
Mom! The alligator ate that bird!;

until at the ocean's edge, we are warned
of powerful waves, strong currents, riptides and man-o'-war.

Friends ask, "How was your vacation?"

Florida has an edge, I reply,
Florida has an edge.

Gently Goodbye

The older I get
the more me and the earth
are doing this little dance.

I'm standing up straight,
next minute leaning to the right,
sometimes the left,
then forward like I'm bowing
at the end of a tune.

I always thought I'd leave
like an old tree in a wind storm,
but I'm just me
with breath from the other side
rocking me back and forth
toward a sleep

where my dreams
of turning into a bird,
a fawn, a leaf in the sunlight
begin their journey into this world
that is kissing me gently goodbye.

Glory in the Moment

"Tension is who you think you should be.
Relaxation is who you are." - Chinese proverb

If I had an ambitious drive
to express the talents I have inside,
I believe my life would truly be
more exciting than it is to me.

A stirring speech on animal rights,
a serenade in the darkest of nights,
a syndicated radio show,
a platform to share all the things I know.

Instead I lead a quiet life
far from a world of speed and strife.
Without the drive to join the fray,
I seem to hold the world at bay.

At night I climb into my bed,
my cat pressed softly against my leg,
review my day and often assess
I could have done better, maybe the best.

A talk show on NBC,
a country band on MTV,
my poems read at inaugurations,
medals won in competitions.

Instead I clean my house, arrange my papers,
read about others and their great adventures,
speak my mind to those I meet
as I walk down our small main street.

With more of a drive I'd have fortune and fame,
at least for a while a household name,
though somewhere inside a voice gentle not rough
is convincing me enough is enough.

Walking through meadows, under budding new trees,
watching clouds float in a soft summer's breeze,
swimming in rivers as the sun is setting,
grateful for days of giving and getting.

The bees within flowers,
rain in spring showers,
live their lives fully through sacred hours.

"Don't listen," they say, "to your self-serving stories.
Being alive is the attainment of glory."

I Believe

I believe

... an imprisoned orangutan throwing a tangerine at a spectator is doing the right thing;

... other species organizing and taking the world back from humans would be a case of justice served;

... dancing on one foot while balancing a broom on one's nose and twirling a chainsaw in one's left hand indicates an unusual use of one's time;

... trying to ice skate when one has no sense of balance and an advanced state of osteoporosis is a bad idea;

... creating images of Jesus by scraping a piece of burnt toast shows a type of devotion particular to bread lovers;

... people volunteering to be sent into outer space to distant planets have no idea what they are getting themselves into;

... splicing canine and feline genes into the human genome would be helpful;

... speciesism is the basis of all prejudice and is practiced by almost all humans;

... some ideas of celebrated Western male philosophers are common sense or wrong;

... all beings share a common cosmic consciousness and intelligence;

... junk food should cost more that healthy food;

... those who feel money is paramount should eat it for lunch and dinner;

... skipping down the street is an acceptable mode of adult transportation;

... animals are aware of death;

... a free public service should be available to help people face their fears;

... anyone objecting to government programs should not receive any benefits from them;

... we all need to recognize the oppressor within;

... horseradish should be a staple in American cuisine;

... meat eaters should witness the killing of the animals they eat;

... whoever declares war should be the only ones fighting.

It's a Match!

On the first night of our vacation,
I'm scrounging around the beach
picking up endless scraps of plastic
while my twin happily breathes in
the sweet sea air and admires the sunset.

The fourth morning we wake
to find the cat missing.
I'm convinced he's injured or dead.
My sister assumes he's fine.

On a train ride, I'm worried I bought
the wrong tickets and we'll be kicked off the train
one stop short of where our relatives are waiting.
She believes it will all work out.

Our flight home is delayed.
Oh no! We'll be trapped in the airport,
miss work and lose money.
Morgan reads and snacks.

Our senses of humor
on the other hand?

A perfect match.

It's Time to Go

The sea says,
"It's time to go,"
and lifts me gently
onto the shore

before waves so huge
no one can swim
crash and slam,
mercy no more.

This gift she gave,
it's time to go,
her love I feel,
her voice I know.

Lightening Up

Credit card receipts flutter to the floor like dry autumn leaves, the ones she's kept just in case. She's so tight with money it strangles her world, but that is changing in this first act of so what as she rakes those receipts into a recycling bag without a second thought. "This is it," she says, ready to leave though she doesn't know when or for that matter where.

The novels from high school from 40 years ago are on the top shelf and she knows she's not ready to say goodbye to them. She loves those books and her ancient margin notes in scared backward-slanting letters remind her she actually understood them—Camus's *The Stranger,* Virginia Woolf's *To the Lighthouse,* Upton Sinclair's *The Jungle.* She breathes in the pages from so long ago. No, she can never give those books away. But these others, untouched for years. No more packing them and staggering to a moving truck.

And these boxes of letters and cards from lovers, family, friends, students, the ones she pictures reading in her old age to reassure herself she was once connected, loving and loved. Won't she need them if her eyes hold up and she can actually read, if she can still remember the people who signed them? This is going to be hard, she thinks, that fire in the backyard offering up the past as smoke to the gods.

And this softball glove she wore one late summer afternoon when she ran barely touching the ground and leapt high into the air to catch a fly ball, nothing in that moment but the ball and her outstretched hand. She hovered, she knows she did, a split second at the top of that arc as free as she had ever been or ever would be again before the descent back into the world and the one step after another that have led her to this moment.

Yes, that is the feeling she is moving toward, that lightness from leaving the weight of her history, of everything but her own body, behind. Maybe then she can rise again like an angel, untethered, if only for a few seconds. What a gift that would be.

Like a Deer

The leaves of hemlocks
on the far side of the hill
suspend sunlight
in clear pearls of water.

From the tip of my tongue
these jewels glide
gently down my throat.

I drink from these trees
like a deer
quiet and grateful.

The sunlight wanes.

Nestled among the shadows
of moonlit trees,
I hear her breath first,
then the crack of small branches,
then her tongue licking liquid
from tiny green leaves.

Here we are together
in the darkness
held in a soft summer night.

Love Affair

My first two-wheel bike is a stripped-down,
aquamarine hand-me-down,
dragged out of the garage of a family friend,
deposited in our backyard.

With adoring eyes
I gaze upon this coming of a messiah
with its promise of freedom and salvation.

I walk the bike reverently
through our long backyard,
out the white wooden gate,
and, after a wobble or two,
am gliding in circles.

In the winter, I ride around the basement.
In the summer, I ride from the backyard
to the front to play hopscotch,
then for hours through our sleepy, safe town.

What perfect speed! How smooth!
Even when the gearshift falls into the front wheel
flinging me over the handlebars onto the sidewalk,
I do not lose one molecule of enthusiasm.

This wonder takes me away from the house,
gives me wings, a breeze through my hair,
a sense of control over my life, and the feeling
that someday I could ride out of this small town
into a world of possibility.

Me and the Antenna

Cool rain pierces the heat of day.
Thunderclouds burst from the west
sending gusts of pine needles
and twigs over houses and along the ground.

My head is bare,
the headband holding my thoughts together
blown under the lawn chair.

I watch for a bolt from the universe,
me and the antenna atop my house
our arms outstretched

as twigs form patterns at my feet
like tea leaves at the bottom
of an offered cup.

Moments

Queen Anne's Lace
galaxies in the moonlight

The lullaby sings itself to sleep

Shattered birch limbs
bones on the forest floor

Groundless
each moment
a step onto a lily pad

Strong breezes
archeologist's brushes
sweep sand away grain by grain

Young men so fit and strong pull in smoke
not knowing someday they will be like that old man
pulling oxygen behind him in a suitcase

White whales pilgrimage
to sacred sands
scraping off all attachments

Homeopathy pills roll
from their container like eggs
from the backside of a turtle

The model sits surrounded
students staring at her
then at their sculptures
creating statues that look
exactly like themselves

Liquid lines of thought across the page

Nipper the Zipper and Howdy Tattoo

Nipper the Zipper and Howdy Tattoo
go sailing one day in a boat made of glue.
They don't get very far. They're stuck where they are.

"What shall we do?" asks Howdy Tattoo.

"Can't say," mumbles Zip,
"the glue's got my lip!"

A dolphin swimming gently nearby
sees this big mess and gives out a cry.

"I'll help you gladly, I always do,
if you'll never again make a ship out of glue.

"We promise, we promise, we give you our word,
as best as we can, if we can be heard."

The dolphin smiles and knows it is true:
if she takes them out of that gooey glue,
they would see how smart those who swim can be
and devote their lives to protecting the sea.

And here's what happened from her good action
in Howdy and Zipper's amazing reaction:
they now walk the beaches combing the shore
picking up garbage wherever they are!

No Escape

no escape
no escape
no escape
at all

landmines
craters
ashes
bones
I'm reeling
from the fall

in this landscape
no escape
no escape
at all

No Guilt There

I take the dachshunds for a walk,
knowing my friend with a bum knee
and aversion to movement,
rarely gives these dogs
the exercise they need.

On with the leashes and the little ones, tails up,
prance out the front door and down the driveway.

A quick turn to the left, a pounce into the bushes,
a surprised squeal, and the dog's head pops back out
with a dead baby bird in her mouth.

Dropping it, she walks nonchalantly away.

Only in My Dreams

Tonight starts with a chase,
unseen enemies close behind,
running at great speed down a dark street,
then into a hotel lobby to buy some time.

A voluptuous woman,
flesh cascading over a black sleeveless dress,
glides past me into the dining room
leaving her afterimage in the dim lobby light.

My eyes dart looking for escape,
a crouch and a jump to the top
of the vaulted ceiling.

Waking, I plod to the bathroom,
knees creaking, to warm myself
in an early morning shower.

Our Nature Walk

Our assigned guide through a Floridian ecosystem is new at the job and, though she knows a lot, there are certain gaps in her knowledge. Perhaps that's why, out of the blue, a young woman with long purple-red hair and an encyclopedic knowledge of flora and fauna joins us when the tour begins.

As we take our first few steps down the trail, someone asks our older guide if there are snakes or any other creatures we should be wary of. Before she can answer, the younger one jumps in and tells us the creatures we should fear the most are right there at our feet, fire ants that can crawl up our legs, bite, and create extreme and prolonged pain. She then kneels down and lets one climb onto her hand, a big security ant with paranoid tendencies whose mission in life is to protect the anthill. She notes its unusually large size and tells us of parasites that enter ants' bodies, mature and explode out of the top of the ants' heads.

Segueing seamlessly, she mentions shark attacks and explains that sharks attack humans because they mistake them for seals. "You can be swimming along calmly," she says, "but your silhouette from below resembles a seal and sharks will go for your midsection. If they happen to chomp down on only your arm or leg, they won't continue to feed because what they really want is a seal."

Suddenly she vanishes and then pops right back in front of us holding a curly tailed lizard, which she says has just been engaged in a battle with a much larger lizard for territorial privileges. The little captive is gazing into our eyes as our guide lets us know she and others have been given orders to kill these lizards upon contact. Fortunately for us all, she doesn't perform an execution, but releases the little one into the underbrush.

Meandering on, we come to a vine that is yellow-orange, leafless, and strangling everything it comes into contact with. "This is called the love vine," she says, "which is appropriate since love strangles and you can love someone to death."

The older guide is trying to normalize the narrative, but I am really enjoying the unusual tone this nature walk has taken and find it inspires parallel explanations on my part. "Watch out," I tell my sister. "These berries pop off so fast, they can take your eyes out. And the shells of these underbrush turtles? They explode like manhole covers and can knock you to the ground."

We continue our climb through this Floridian landscape that peaks at 14 feet surrounded by animal and plant life that could in reality or imagination cause unexpected damage. Pelicans and storks glide above us as prehistoric and elegant as their ancient ancestors. With life pulsing in front and back, below and above us, I am struck by how thin the veneer of human civilization is—how Floridian roads and buildings need constant attention, that if not tended to they would soon be covered in vines, with countless birds and reptiles living in the luxury condos.

This vision is intriguing, humbling and thrilling, much like our nature walk now coming to an end at the air-conditioned nature center and steaming parking lot.

Overheard in a Bus Terminal

—I should've bought those scratch tickets! I need that money and I blew it!

—How do you know you would've won?

—I was on a roll. The game was Play Five! It was my fifth ticket. I won five dollars. The guy was reaching for the next five tickets. I can't believe I took the five for the toll out of town!

—A lot of people take the money.

—I always go for the small stuff! It's like it's the 1930s and I'm saving every little piece of string!

—Well, actually, you do. Remember that huge ball in your basement?

—I've explained that!

—You never said how you'd be at home when the world falls apart.

—Forget it, okay?

—Listen, your Buddhist practice needs to kick in. Be happy for the person who won. Maybe they need it more than you do.

—I've tried! I keep picturing that old man in the corner. Maybe he won.

—Listen, let's get something to eat. It's on me.

—Really?!

—Yeah, just give me half your winnings next time, okay?

—Okay, whatever you say, man.

Put That On

—Honey, put that blouse on.

—No.

—Put it on now.

—No.

—You can't go to camp with no shirt on, so put it on right now.

—Boys don't wear shirts!

—Well, girls do. They need protection!

—I don't. I can beat up the boys.

—Honey, I told you not to do that. It makes them feel bad.

—I feel bad.

—Well, it's time to put that aside. You've gotta wear a shirt to camp and a dress to school and that's it. End of story. Now put that shirt on.

—No. No shirt. No school. No nothin'.

—You know, when I was your age I felt the same way, but some things are more powerful than us. It's easier when you look like everyone else.

—Everybody else can look like me.

—Listen, at least put on an undershirt. The neighbors are starting to complain. Their girls want to go without shirts too.

—Really? Who?

—No names. All I'm saying is you're becoming a bad example. Now put it on.

—Okay, close your eyes and tell me what's for supper.

—Salad, minute steaks, baked potato, string beans. Ready? She's gone! Harold! Adele's gone! She's run out the back door. Without a shirt!

—Coming, coming. Okay, you go that way this time and bring the clothes with you.

—Oh my God! There she is! See her, Harold? On the Virgin's head! This is it! She's waving to Mrs. Danfer! I can't believe it! She's gone feral!

—Calm down, sweetie. Adele, come down now.

—Nope.

—Right now.

—Nope.

—I have a baseball mitt for you.

—What?

—You heard me. Come down and put on the shirt. Yes or no?

—Okay.

—Good girl.

—Harold, you always give in to her. Always. She's never gonna learn.

—Well, we'll see Mama. Remember how you looked in that football uniform on Halloween? Maybe she's gonna grow up to be just like you.

Questions

Does a race horse ever hurry?

Why do people love to go to boxing matches
and watch people punch each other in the face?

Doesn't a Puritan society,
which values work over pleasure,
have to create problems in order to keep everyone busy?

When I see the sun rise,
why don't I remember its light has just slid across the Atlantic?

Why is the litter along roads always beer cans,
soda bottles, cigarette butts, and junk food wrappers,
not coconut water bottles and empty bags of tofu snacks?

Why do so many middle-aged American men
look like they are four to eight months pregnant?

Isn't repetitive thinking like a mono-crop
of the brain?

If the results from "experimenting" on animals
were transferrable to humans,
why don't we go to veterinarians?

Where do the socks go? Really!

Ramon Sampedro

Ramon Sampedro,
in a moment of distraction,
dove into the sea and broke his neck.

He could move only his head
and tongue as he lay in bed
in his brother's house in Spain
writing beautiful poetry
with a pencil at the end of a stick
held in his mouth.

He fought to die,
to release the heavy anchor of his body
tended day after day by women
who fell in love with him,
as he watched the sun rise and set,
light and weather change,
outside his window.

For thirty years
no one would help him die
until one woman loved him so much
she lifted the liquid to his lips
and set him free.

The Real Problem

Chem trails crisscross
the air above Taos
turning the famous clear blue
New Mexican sky hazy most days,
sickening the people.

Letters have been written to the editor.
Groups have been formed.

The resident response so far
has been not to the chem trails
but to the unsightliness
of the protest signs along the road.

The Show Must Go On

It was to be the opening night of my show, which had been heralded as cutting edge and a must-see for the St. Paul-Minneapolis avant-garde. I had been wary of the advance publicity and let my reputation from former performances carry the moment, as I too shared the great speculation, having decided to merely accumulate a number of props and improvise.

These were no regular props however. One was a rusted-out car from 1963 given to me by friends north of Bemidji. Another was a bottle of water taken from where the Mississippi River began and another bottle of water from where it ended in New Orleans. I also had a snowball flown in from the northernmost part of Alaska in a transplant organ bag and a lava carving from a Polynesian island carried on a Kon-Tiki like raft built especially for the show.

I knew I could make it all work and was letting ideas roll around my mind as I was driving up from Chicago, until I was jolted into reality by what I thought were drums but was actually the sound of the tread separating from my front wheel tire. I pulled over in a state of anxiety and contemplated my situation. How would I get to St. Paul in time with a large chunk of Chicago sidewalk in the trunk, my fragile baby blanket riding shotgun, and only an hour and a half until setup and final orientation to the stage? I chose to flag down an oil delivery truck by standing in the middle of the road and refusing to move.

The driver was a 50-year-old woman on the second shift of her third job and she was not happy. I begged. I pleaded. I promised her $1,000 and a role in the show. I was lucky. She had had it and had actually been thinking of turning her truck around and heading for Arizona. So after pondering my proposal for about five minutes, she made a few phone calls and then threw the chunk of sidewalk behind the truck seats. I grabbed my blanket, called AAA to get the car, and we rolled right up to St. Paul and the stage entrance with time to spare.

You might have heard of this woman or seen her on Oprah Winfrey. She calls herself Gus after her character in that first show when she received rave reviews and shot to the front page of the New York Times Entertainment Section. Since then, she's had great success as a performance artist and motivational speaker.

I ride with her now and then from town to town in that original oil truck, which the Smithsonian has expressed an interest in. We give impromptu performances on street corners, though I spend most of my creative life providing props for Hollywood movies and New York plays. I continue to develop a deep trust in the ways of the universe, which I did not have before this incident, so that when I stall on the road of life, I do believe the universe will indeed provide.

Small Jersey Town, 1960

We do not speak the truth.

We choose lies,
postures of deference,

look for cues,
abandon exuberance,

all us girls in unwanted dresses
and shoes that bind.

Softball!

Yeah, I'm that kind of athlete.
Sweep to the side, ball straight in the pocket,
fly dropping in
like iron
to a magnet.

The wooden bat,
a beautiful sound,
a slide so fast,
a gentle push,
back on my feet,
safe on the bag.

Catch at first,
then a shot to third,
straight lines, perfect arcs.
Don't need a math class to figure that out.

And then when world fades away,
just me, the ball, the glove,
a leap in the air,
suspended in space, in silence
before dropping down into this life
with the next thing that needs to be done.

Those seconds last a lifetime.

Like I said, I'm that kind of athlete.
A thoroughbred.
A bird.

Spinning Thoughts

Thoughts like Lionel toy trains
circle endlessly on little tracks

through the same villages,
past the same tiny trees,
over the same bridges,
with the same people
waving in the exact same spots,

the conductor
manipulating different levers,
unaware she is being driven
by remote control.

Traversing an unchanging landscape,
she spins around every curve
looking expectantly ahead,
as if the terrain she is entering
were new and she in charge.

Stanley and the Birth of the Universe

Driving around in bumper cars and trying to smash into Stanley made for a strange first date, but then, Stanley was strange. His uniqueness, it turned out, was an irresistible pheromone to many women, myself included. Everything about his appearance was average: average height, brown hair, brown eyes, trim but not muscular, a nice smile, but not one that knocked you off your feet. It was his far-reaching mind that was amazing, a mind that started one place and ended light years away. People who chose to take that trip with him were fascinated and most followed his logic until his final leap into an idea that very few had even considered.

"I was right there with you," they would say, "but I came to a totally different conclusion!" And it was no different that night when everyone offered some version of that reaction, but not me—which is how he and I ended up in bumper cars on the infield of a NASCAR training track in a small town in Georgia.

Six women and two men were on this writing retreat, each in isolation in individual cabins for ten days, meals delivered to our front doors. I had met Stanley the first day at orientation and had been thinking about him on and off during those days of writing. I had even written a short story based on who I imagined him to be—a trapeze trainer afraid of heights—a story you can actually read in the October 1997 issue of *The New Yorker*.

Anyway, I found out Stanley had been thinking of me and had written a story with a character based on who he thought I could be: a dominatrix who had given up the S & M scene to become a nurturer of orphaned baby elephants in Africa. That one was never published.

Well, when all eight of us emerged from our cabins and reconvened in the main hall for a banquet and the reading of our work, I found myself seated next to Stanley and a flirtation began immediately. I told him about my fantasy of him and he jokingly asked if I had a stash of whips and black leather. Our amusement with each other turned to talk about the nature of amusement itself and then more literally about amusement parks, at which point the workshop leader mentioned the carnival one town over. After putting out a general invitation and getting no takers, Stanley got down on one knee and asked me to ride the bumper cars with him. It was one of the most thrilling offers I had had in a long time. What innovative sublimation and way to work off all that mental energy!

So off we went, Stanley and me, to crash into each other at increasingly unique angles, then spinning away and ricocheting off the walls as people gathered around, strangely fascinated. The most amazing thing, though, was that Stanley was writing a poem in his head as all of this was going on, a poem that is still being taught not only in most poetry classes around the country, but in theoretical astrophysics classes as well. He entitled it "Bumper Cars and the Birth of the Universe," and it speaks of love, angles, collisions, sparks, and speeds in such a way that its language has been adopted in scientific circles to describe astral phenomena.

As Einstein said, "Logic will get you from A to B. Imagination will take you everywhere." The proof of this can be seen in Stanley's far-flung connections which have united poets, mystics, and scientists and created the universe we two have now shared for almost a lifetime, whatever that is.

There Is a Sadness

There is a sadness without limits,
a joy that has no bounds.
They live within each other.
They share a common ground.

Grief is a shadow
that floats within the light.
Beauty holds the loss of all
within its blackest night.

I've tried to live with one of these
and wandered lost alone.
Embracing all I've found within
our sacred common home.

Tompkins Square II

First Prize Story as told at the Greenfield Annual Word Festival, Greenfield MA, October 2015

It is 1968. The place is the East Village in New York City. This is the height of political revolution and the crowning year for hippies. I was not particularly in the mainstream of hippiedom, but I sort of looked that way. I had long hair and dressed sort of the way that I'm dressed now. This is the neighborhood that has been the home to generation after generation of immigrants. It used to be a Jewish neighborhood and a German neighborhood and, at the time I was there, it was Hispanic. With these types of neighborhoods, often another group starts coming in and the people who live there start to feel threatened. And at this point, it was many Puerto Ricans and a trickle of hippies into that neighborhood.

Many of you can perhaps remember St. Marks Place? Well, this was the beginning when the little Birkenstock stores started and you have the hippies in the window carving leather to weave the sandals and there would be pot shops and bongs and marijuana smell in the air and little cafes for music. Well, there was a lot of tension in that neighborhood.

I was there and I was staying in my sister's apartment. This was a time when there were "railroad" apartments, so you had a bedroom, you had the bathtub in the kitchen, you had the bathroom in the hall, and the rent was about $65 a month. I was staying there and one summer morning

I decided to go down to Tompkins Square Park to relax, a little oasis in the middle of the metropolitan area. I had my little book The Invisible Man by Ralph Ellison. And I go down there, sit in the shade, and I'm sitting with my back to a wall very similar to this.

I'm sitting there and all of a sudden splat! I feel something hit my arm. I look down and there is a dripping rotten apple just sort of oozing toward to the concrete. I do not take being hit lightly, sort of like a little fuse goes off. I'm looking around and I see this young Hispanic boy's face peering at me over the brick wall. I pick up the apple and he takes off and I take off after him. I am running as fast I can. I position myself. I take the apple and *fwat*! get him right square in the middle of his back.

Then I think hmmm perhaps I should leave the park. So I turn around and recover my book and I'm sauntering like this. You know, I have my tough New York walk. It's served me well many times. But all of a sudden, I turn around just to make sure and I see a whole gang coming after me. It's about eight to ten people, ages maybe fourteen and up. But these were the civilized days and what happened was, as I sauntered out of the park, bam! I feel something on the back of my head.

I turn around and they had sent a girl to fight me. It wasn't all the boys. They weren't there with Uzis like it would be now and machetes. They just sent a girl to take the hippie girl down. So, what happened was we started wrestling. I was very strong at the time—the good old days—wrestled her to the ground, pinned her to the ground, and I said, "I don't want to fight. If I let you up, peace." This happened three times when she would jump on me and I'd pin her down.

Finally she was on the ground. I looked up and the leader said, "You can leave the park now. We won't hurt you." Because I had won all the fights. But I couldn't leave the park and I went and I sat on a park bench. The gang sat next to me, the leader was right here. He took out a Kleenex. He wiped my eyes. He tried talking to me about the book. And at some point, he snapped his fingers, the whole gang got up, they all left the park, I cried, and went home.

The reason I want to tell this story is because I think that guy who led that gang was the greatest leader I ever saw. He used appropriate force, he met the enemy, he tried to save honor, he maintained peace, and he honored his enemy. So I salute him wherever he is.

Too Many Words

Too many words colliding,
shattering, dissolving
in their own noise.

The tone of a singing bowl,
surf on pebbles,
warm wood creaking.

Can our words be
as beautiful as that?

The Turkeys Know

The turkeys know
something terrible
happened here.

Clucking, skittish,
they circle the stump,

moving through energy
that eluded the ones
who had cut
that tree
down.

Under the Full Moon

The boy reaches for the carrot in his back pocket just to make sure it is there. It's going to be a long night and his provisions will need to be rationed. He has learned a lot about rationing from his favorite TV shows, which involve some variation of scraggly men stumbling through endless sand dunes with one canteen, men who become delirious, hallucinatory, with swollen tongues seeking shade under the one scrub tree for miles around.

This isn't the boy's circumstance exactly. He is in his backyard in suburban Long Island having convinced his parents that sleeping under a full moon really is a homework assignment from his science teacher who wants to show his students that sleeping under such a moon would cause an increase in their blood flow as measured by the Blood Meter, an invention of the teacher himself.

His mother was quite skeptical, in fact a bit fearful, but did her research and became convinced the device could cause her son no harm. She herself strapped the device around his chest, applied the cuff around his left index finger, and turned the whole contraption on at 8:48 p.m. Her only demand was that she sleep in her own tent next to his in case anything went wrong.

So it comes to be that the boy wakes at two o'clock in the morning to unusual murmurings and mutterings. He peeks out the front flap and sees his next door neighbor, Mr. Perkins, climbing out of his living room window holding a large manila envelope. Close by a man straight out of the mystery shows he loves so much is standing under the Japanese maple. His brimmed hat is pulled down to his eyes and he is large, overweight, and unsmiling. This is so cool, the boy thinks, sort of like those movies his mother calls film noir.

"Ma! Ma, wake up, wake up!" he whispers before seeing two men emerge from the large forsythia bush, tape Mr. Perkins' mouth shut, rope him up like a calf at a rodeo, throw him into the back seat of a car, and head silently out into the night. The large man picks up the manila envelope and nonchalantly makes his way down the sidewalk toward the center of town. The boy stares at the empty space where the men were moments before and pinches himself to see if he is dreaming.

When the police arrive, the boy is still strapped into the Blood Meter, his mother is shaking, and his father is next door sitting on the front steps trying to comfort Mrs. Perkins, who keeps repeating, "I knew something was wrong. I knew something was wrong." The forensics team dusts for fingerprints and searches for fibers and footprints in the soft spring lawn.

The police are incredulous. "A Prius? Are you sure?"

"I'm positive," the boy says. "My friend told me they're the new getaway car 'cause they're so quiet."

II

Looking back, I have to admit the whole Prius percep-
tion was probably inaccurate though I believed it when

I said it. But everything else must have happened, and that night changed my life forever. I'm sorry to say Mr. Perkins was never found. Ever. His wife is still looking and making sure the police keep the case open all these twenty years. I'm really hoping the police find something. For everyone's sake.

As for my old science teacher, I looked him up and found that his Blood Meter has become a huge success. He used the data from his many classes and it did show that blood flow increases significantly and distributes itself differently under the full moon. NASA incorporated his invention into its space program and uses it to monitor the behavior of the circulatory system on space stations. It is, of course, no longer called the Blood Meter. Mr. Calhoun said he named it that in the hope that the students in his seventh grade classes would find it cool and cooperate, but once he had a scientific and economic gold mine on his hands, he changed the name to the Phlebotomy Monitoring System, known jokingly in the aerospace world as PMS. Calhoun never was good at naming things.

Anyway, I was traumatized that night, and to this day I wonder if life itself is just a dream. It is true, we all agree, that Mr. Perkins seems to have vanished permanently, but sometimes I think he staged the whole thing to escape his boring life. I know it was boring because he used to say so when I mowed his lawn. "Kid," he would say, "my life is so boring, watching you mow the lawn is probably as exciting as this day is going to get." But then again, maybe he was setting me up. If what I saw really happened, his life would have been far from boring. This possibility won't let me rest.

Our family moved the next year. I had become so fixated on establishing concrete evidence of Mr. Perkins' kidnapping that I was compulsively going over the entire area with a fine-tooth comb. Literally. My parents decided I needed a change, so we moved to San Francisco. That, I must say, was one excellent outcome, and I'm grateful my formative years were spent in the city of difference, outrageousness, and acceptance, a place where people are obviously making up their own narratives.

I discovered in my philosophy classes at UC Berkeley that humans are making things up all the time and that the best we can hope for is a shared narrative. So I will leave you with this invitation to join mine. If you have any information at all regarding the above-described incident, please contact me, Detective John Murphy, Head of the Bureau of Missing Persons, San Francisco Police Department. I will be forever grateful.

Unfolding Story

Our days and nights
an unfolding story
scrawled on pages
snapping in a storm.

Wisps of a plot,
motives hidden,
words enticing,
confusing, and dark.

I fight comprehension
page after page
as one scene
after another
pulls me inexorably
toward the end.

Vacation Time

As I am preparing for my next-day flight to Florida, I learn that the Zika virus has arrived before me and that thousands of sharks are congregating off Palm Beach, a few miles from where I'd be swimming. Not deterred, I tie up loose ends and head to the airport early to avoid any anxiety, only to find a two-hour delay being stretched into six.

There is absolutely nowhere to go, nothing to do. Fortunately and unexpectedly, I slip into a meditative state worthy of a month-long retreat at a Buddhist monastery. I don't feel fear or impatience. In fact, I don't feel anything at all. I sit. Get up and walk around. Sit and walk some more. Watch people, sit, and walk some more.

Eventually, the plane scheduled to leave at 4:15 is open for boarding at 10 p.m. and we file in and sit through the announcement of a missing fuel cap and the time it takes maintenance to make sure the plane is safe to fly, as snow and sleet, newly arrived in the darkness, accumulate on the wings and against the windows.

Behind me, a woman with a strong New York City accent is announcing her annoyance to the world, yelling repeatedly into her cell phone, "I'm not happy. I'm not happy at all." Then a woman requests to leave what seems like a doomed flight and retreats into the safety of the terminal. Eventually, we roll over to the de-icing station and finally into the air, only to hit turbulence two hours later so rough the plane drops straight down and we are left hovering over our seats while a collective scream fills the plane. The man next to me vomits and the woman next to him pops a tranquilizer.

At 1:00 a.m., I rent a car and wind my way down unknown, dark, deserted highways and streets searching for my sister's condo, and arrive just before torrential rain, heavy winds, and thunder and lightning fill the sky and toss the palm trees, tornadoes to the south, tornadoes to the west.

I awake dazed and happy to be alive, ready to step into the warm, sweet air and the ocean nearby. Approaching the water, my sister and I see a sign: powerful waves, danger: man-o'-war, strong current north. We jump in. It's glorious. In this world, really, what else is there to do?

Walking Away

After he throws her grandmother's washboard
through the old farmhouse window,
she knows her days of trying are over.

She leans against the old barn
gazes at the abandoned trough,
the dust of the last grains on the worn warm wood.

The cacti are blooming,
the desert flowers,
red, yellow, blue jewels
scattered before the mountain gods.

She walks inside, takes the money,
gets a jacket, and in her summer dress
walks down the old dirt road toward town,
the bus station, and rain.

Water Seeks Its Own Level

I
The room is dark,
Kleenex strewn across the floor,
white carnations heavy as lead.

The home health aide
washes the dishes and straightens up,
now and then retiring to the living room
to release her heavy body
into the soft living room chair.

II
She enters my room,
medicated hot water in a bottle,
a tube and receiving pan in hand.

Holding the bottle high,
she lowers the tube toward my mouth
as water gushes into the air and over the bed.

"Water seeks its own level! Water seeks its own level!"
I shout, but it's only the reaching out
of my hand to lift hers that helps.

III
I heal that evening.
The aide does not return.
And water, water continues to seek its own level.

The Wedding

Dear Alexander,

I'm sorry you weren't able to attend Debbie's wedding last week, but we understand that flying in from Benin was asking a lot. I'll just catch you up on what you missed and you can determine if your decision was a good one or not.

We arrived early in case we were needed and it turns out our presence was crucial. The chuppah was set up at the bottom of the steep hill at the High Pines Country Club and the first thing we saw was a group of guests in their seventies and eighties trying to make their way downhill. They were slanting forward at alarming angles and using their walkers and canes just to stay upright. As we rushed over, Mrs. Gronowski actually fell forward, while good old George just sat down and tried to get to his chair by sliding on his derriere! We managed to catch four guests before any more catastrophes happened!

When everyone was seated, a rumor circulated that the bride, who, as you know, is usually late, hadn't arrived yet. This turned out to be true and the guests, generally dry to begin with, baked under the sun for an hour before the music started and Deb, still beautiful at 48, slowly made her way down the hill with Jon behind.

Then Rabbi Kaplan finally began a beautiful service. I must admit it is difficult for me to remember much after her first few sentences because Deb was signaling to her husband-to-be and actually mouthing words while the rabbi was conducting the ceremony! Rabbi Kaplan, the amazing woman that she is, forged on and Deb and Jon managed to get married. Then the trek back up the hill began.

Most of guests made a successful climb. I'm told they gulped down every glass of water on every tray and table they could find. Mr. Bergman, who had been a mountain climber in his younger days, was the first to arrive and wasn't even out of breath. Mr. Gruen, on the other hand, who had spent his life in retail, was in bad shape and we had to stop every few steps to administer an electrolyte mixture just to keep him going, but even he made it, and the festivities with great music and delicious catered food began.

This wedding was, to say the least, a bit different from your father's and my potluck wedding all those years ago. We were so young and hopeful then. We actually believed walking blindfolded through a pasture helping each other avoid cow paddies was a great way to begin a marriage. For all I know, Deb and Jon will do a lot better than us because their meshugas, as they say, is on the surface and their flare-ups burn off quickly.

Anyway, I miss you and thank the world every day that you were born. It would have been fun if you had been there, but maybe I've given you a good enough picture so it feels like you really were by my side.

Lots of love always,
Mom

What If

What if
  I stopped worrying
    … embraced being kind as life's deepest meaning
    … saw more of the humor in this world

        What if
          I lived in the present
            … felt safe
              … gave up the story of my life

What if
  I could run a mile
    … accept life as it is
      … be full of gratitude

        What if
          I knew when I was going to die
            … were rooted in the beauty of the world
              … fell in love one more time

What They Can Do

It is ironic
words I love
bring me to darkness
thick and black
where only silence
brings me back.

Words can save,
words can heal,
can keep a mind on even keel,
or toss that mind in storms at sea
and not allow a soul to be.

Whatever

Whenever they wonder whatever to do,
knowing now once was then
and what once was who,
she answers their questions
wherever they are, whenever the plea,
of however, whoever she thinks they can be:

"You were given a clue to whatever you knew,
so whoever may ask, whenever they do,
say you live by whatever you know to be true,
and wherever the thought of however ensues,
don't abandon whatever, whatever you do."

WHUT *Present Time*

Hello to all our WHUT listeners and welcome to our live broadcast of Present Time. We are outside the apartment house of "Half-Pinky" Petrozini, known as Muffles, who was arrested here at 312 Maple Street five years ago. We are offering a unique prize this year.

As you know, mafia kingpin Petrozini was identified by our local dentist Dr. Swartzberg who had read about the tiny tattoo on the inside of Petrozini's right cheek. The arrest was made when Muffles was brought to his office after being accidentally hit in the mouth with a stapler by an accountant at Bob's Tax Return.

To honor this event, the 22nd visitor to our booth will receive a free plastic surgery consultation with the doctor who created a completely different appearance for the most wanted man in America. Anyone in our listening audience who has ever wanted to look like someone else is encouraged to come down for a shot at this amazing opportunity. Remember, the 22nd visitor. 312 Maple Street. And now a word from our sponsors.

The following are excerpts from the first interview given to
WHUT by Petrozini after his incarceration.

Why the name Muffles?

I like the play on words, you know, keeping quiet, flyin' under the radar, muffler. So Muffles popped into my head. But thinkin' about it, there was this girl in sixth grade with a stuffed doll named Muffles. I loved that girl, but she didn't love me. I used to lie in bed and imagine

Maria was holdin' me. So that had somethin' to do with it too. Sentimental coming from a crook like me, but who cares. My life's over. I wanna get everything off my chest.

Why did you maintain your disguise even when you were sleeping?

I wanted to be a famous actor once and studied The Method way of actin'. You familiar with that? You get into your character 'n live like your character until you become 'em. Well, I decided Muffles was a non-descript kind of guy, yuh know, but quirky. So I was developin' the quirky side of my character that night I got arrested. You know, the panda pajamas. Bad timing.

Where does the nickname "Half-Pinky" come from as your pinkies are intact?

That was my callin' card. Anyone who crossed me was left with half a pinky. Everyone knows that. I was proud of how good I was doin' what needed to be done in a professional way.

How does it feel to look so different?

Well, yuh know, I was once the handsomest guy in the whole East Coast Mafia. I could give you the name of 20 women, wife included, who would swear to that. But honestly, I felt they loved me for my looks, so it was sort of a relief when I transformed into a schlub, a real schlub. But I always kept my six-pack. It's beautiful. The paunch was all fake. Wanna try punching me right here? No?

Well, after the plastic surgeries, I felt more like myself. An ordinary guy on the outside but me on the inside. Psychological, right? I've been readin' a lot of psychology lately.

Why didn't you take the plea agreement?

I couldn't rat on my family, my friends. How could I live with myself? Anyway, they would've killed me and besides I got a conscience. If someone gets caught on their own, that's their doin'. I don't want no part of that. And I'm tired. I've been Petrozini. I've been Muffles. I don't wanna be somebody else in a Witness Protection Program. It's okay in here. I'm taking a meditation course 'n workin' with a prison theater troupe. Maybe I'll find peace of mind. Maybe my acting career will take off.

Looking back on your life, what's the biggest lesson you learned?

The big one was to let it all go. I didn't and it cost me big. I wanted to keep a little piece of my life and that tiny tattoo? It was the face of the dog I loved the best. He was only one I ever trusted 'n I wanted to keep him close. I never had a cavity or cleaning in my whole life. No mouth problems. Who knew that little accountant couldn't control his stapler? The lesson is yuh never know what's gonna happen, so prepare for everything, prepare to give up everything. That's the lesson I learned.

You can read more of our interview with "Half-Pinky" Petrozini at WHUT.com.

Winter of Dreams

From a nest of quilts,
I rappel
into a
wondrous
world.

"Don't sleep
your life away,"
I'm told,
but I smile

as lids gently lower
like curtains
in a theater's
dimming
light.

Worlds Within Worlds

After sitting meditation, each person shares their practice, plans, concerns, feelings, and experiences. I describe being in New Mexico and seeing worlds within worlds within worlds: the Universe holding the Earth, the Earth holding the Rio Grande Gorge, the Gorge holding the river, the river holding the hot springs, the hot springs holding me, me holding my mind.

The contrast between my small worried world and the vastness became clear while I was floating in the hot springs, imagining myself becoming tinier and tinier as I climb toward the top of the gorge gazing back at myself in the pool below.

New Mexico is perfect for feeling tiny. Walking the western rim of the Gorge and seeing huge boulders piled up the long, deep slopes carved by the thin river far below as it dug itself deeper and deeper into the earth helped me feel like the speck I actually am, a speck as vast a universe to the atoms within me as starry space is to me.

Now in the meditation room, I realize that everything the person sitting across from me is talking about—her schedule, plans for the day, challenges and worries— exists only in her head and that all the heads in the room are holding their own universes and that the agitation in my brain as I lie awake under the vast New Mexico night sky, as I watch the sun lighten the mesa from behind the Sangre de Cristo mountains, is all made up. Suddenly, for a moment, I understand what Buddhists have been teaching for millennia—that we humans conflate our story lines

and the presence that holds them and confuse the confla-
tion with the world.

Worry

I'm a professional worrier. I can worry anytime, night or day, about the present, past, or future. I really find my groove at 3 a.m. when, dreaming perhaps about wandering through the streets of an ancient city, I'm suddenly awake staring into the darkness, certain I will become a bag lady on the beaches of Miami. There I am at seventy-five living in a cardboard box near the boardwalk or maybe in the huge sandcastle I reconstruct everyday with the broken plastic shovel I've found at low tide. Or I'm on the Boston Commons with a sandwich board announcing I have no job and asking if someone, anyone, would buy my books or CDs so I can return home to pay my mortgage before the bank repossesses my home.

I've been looking for solutions. I've taken to chanting *nam myoho renghe kyo* to establish new neural pathways. I've taken to tapping the top of my head and my face and chest while reciting self-affirmations. These are fruitful developments in a way, since now I have more to worry about, like am I a public nuisance and will I be allowed to roam free and unsupervised.

www.ingramcontent.com/pod-product-compliance
Lightning Source LLC
Chambersburg PA
CBHW021930170626
46807CB00007B/3048